HOW TO DO THINGS YOUR PHONE WON'T:

A COMMON-SENSE GUIDE TO REAL LIFE.

By David Lastinger

How to do things your phone wont:
A common-sense guide to real life

Copyright. 2018 by David Lastinger. All Rights Reserved.

No part of this publication may be reproduced, stored in a retrieval system or transmitted in any means, electronic, mechanical, photocopy, recording or otherwise without the prior permission of the author except as provided by USA copyright law.

Publisher: CreateSpace Independent Publishing
Cover and interior art by Jill Shepherd
Editor: Laura Orsini

ISBN-13: 978-1985897755
ISBN-10: 198589775X

First Edition August 2018

Acknowledgements

There are a number of people that I need to thank for helping me put this book together.

Linda Burridge, my life coach, for spurring me on from the beginning. Your insight has been priceless.

Beth George, Carri Kaufman, and Katy Engels from the Glendale Chamber of Commerce for keeping the spark going.

Molly, Shannon, Traci, and Linda for being my beta readers and providing fantastic feedback.

Laura Orsini, my editor, for putting up with my first-time author questions.

Jill Shepherd, your patience with me as I learned what I was supposed to do and not supposed to do was fantastic.

I am available for speaking engagements. Please contact me directly for more information at dlastinger@yahoo.com

Introduction

These days it seems that we rely on the internet and social media more and more, trusting blindly that what we read will be true, accurate, and in our best interests.

Unfortunately, that's not always the case, and the real world still exists beyond your smartphone. Plain and simple, there are some things your smartphone can't do and social media cannot fix.

We are about to discuss some of those things. I can't guarantee I will cover everything you didn't know, but then again, I don't know what you don't know.

One question you should always ask yourself is this: "Who is **they**"? They told me this, *they* told me that. In the movie, *The Big Short*, the writers and producers actually explain who "they" is and why/how they started – or significantly contributed to – the big real estate crash of 2008.

It is important to take into account those **they** factors, as well as other considerations, when making important decisions. Quite often, **they** don't know your entire financial situation or haven't seen the entire picture, yet you rely on them to help you make crucial financial choices or life-changing decisions.

Seems a little half-assed to me, not to mention irresponsible consulting, on their part.

Online and television financial gurus are famous for this. Sure, they may have some good points and theories, but you should never take their suggestions 100 percent blindly. I suggest you view them, instead, as one more tool in your Life Skills Toolbox.

Even if you have a pricey education or are in the process of achieving one right now, it will most certainly be helpful to take a class on personal financial management or consumer math. Fancy math classes like calculus and trigonometry will not teach you how to balance your checkbook or read a bank statement.

Table of Contents

Section I – Personal Awareness and Safety
    Always Be Aware of Your Surroundings...................7
    Take a Self-Defense Class 9
    CPR and Other First Aid...10
    Gun Safety 11

Section II – Common Sense About Your Car
    Getting Pulled Over by the Police...........................14
    Changing a Tire...16
    Car Emergency Kit..19
    Driving and Technology..20
    Changing Lanes 21
    Texting and Driving 22
    GPS and Navigation Systems 23
    When You're Paying Someone Else to Drive 24

Section III – Common Sense Around the House
    Home Preparedness 27
    Your Medicine Cabinet..29
    Grocery Shopping 31
    Setting Up Your Kitchen...33
    Ready, Set, Cook!..35
    Fire Extinguishers and Smoke Alarms 37
    Pest Control and Creepy Crawlies 39

Section IV – Common Sense About Your Money
    The Importance of Credit..42
    Car Payments versus Housing Payments 44
    Budgets and Spending 46
    Tipping...48
    Hiring Contractors, Mechanics, and
    Other Service Providers..51

Section V – General Life Skills
    Trade School or University?....................................54
    Common Courtesy and Manners.............................56
    Volunteering..58
    Pet Care...60
Wrapping Up...61

Personal Awareness and Safety

Always Be Aware of Your Surroundings

NEWS FLASH: Bad guys exist and will probably continue to exist for as long as you live. Unfortunately, their job in life is to disrupt yours in whatever way possible for their financial – or other – gain. This could come in the form of a carjacking, robbery, purse snatching, or identity theft. You can hope it will never happen to you – but the likelihood is that it will at some point in your life.

You see it on the news all the time. The victim never thought it would happen to them – only to other people, strangers, anyone but themselves or people they know.

It is extremely important to be aware of your surroundings at all times – and though I hate to say it, especially if you are a female and alone.

What are the most likely places for these types of events to occur?

- Parking lots
- ATM locations
- While on a run in the park or hitting the local trails
- Any other place you might find yourself alone with your guard down

How can you reduce your chances of becoming a victim? And how should you respond if something like this were to occur?

- Thieves target people who are distracted, which is exactly what you are when your attention is focused on that little screen in your hand. Stop playing with your phone while heading to your car. If whatever you are doing on the phone is not important to your safety, put it away until you get to a safer place.
- Walk confidently with your head held up and with a little urgency in your step.

- Take a look around and behind you every once in a while to check your surroundings. Keep in mind, the bad guys want easy prey –if you look like you are not paying attention, that could be you.

- Leave one of your ear buds out so you can also hear what is going on around you: traffic, cyclists, bad guys, etc. With music available at the touch of a button, there's no limit to what you can listen to on your phone via a multitude of apps. Many people have become so accustomed to doing this on a walk, a run, or during a workout in a public place. I'm not telling you to abandon the tunes – just be smart about it.

- Get your keys out before you reach the door of your car. Don't spend time fumbling to look for them.

- For added security, look around your car before you approach it to be certain no one is hiding on the other side.

If you do get a weird feeling about someone near your car, just keep walking and head back to the store or wherever you came from. It is perfectly okay to ask a security guard or employee to escort you to your car. Most employees will be happy to do it.

Take a Self-Defense Class

Ideally, you should take a personal self-defense class from a qualified instructor. Classes can be found in a number of places. Your local community college, a martial arts studio, or your gym might offer them. They are generally quite affordable, if you consider what you get in return. Check out the options available in your area and find one that works for you.

Taking such a class will give you confidence so that if someone does happen to accost you, you will know what to do and have the skills to defend yourself. You might also find that you enjoy a particular martial art style so much that it becomes a part of your regular workout routine. Bonus!

If you decide to carry a weapon for self-protection, it's important that you get properly trained and obtain any licenses that go along with that. Ongoing practice with your weapon of choice should become a regular habit for you. In the event that you ever need to use your weapon, doing so should come second nature to you. Respond first and think about it later.

Whether you choose to arm yourself is strictly a personal decision, and you should feel comfortable with your choice. You are dealing with your safety and/or that of your family.

CPR and Other First Aid

Now that you are out on your own, it's a good idea to get some general first aid and CPR training. You never know what might happen to you, your friends, or strangers you meet along the way. A first aid class will give you the knowledge and skills to help if you ever find yourself in such a situation. It's a terrible feeling to witness an emergency as a mere bystander.

I am not a doctor, so I won't offer any medical advice here. But there are techniques you can learn that could save a life one day.

An extremely reputable source for first aid and CPR training is the American Red Cross. This organization is recognized worldwide and does a great job of this sort of training. If there is not a branch in your city or town, perhaps your local community college or parks & recreation department will have a class.

While it is possible to learn some of these first aid skills online, there is nothing like getting that hands-on training from a real-life instructor. He or she will be able to watch your technique to be certain you have mastered it, rather than guessing from the video. For instance, the pace of your compressions can matter greatly when it comes to saving a life with CPR.

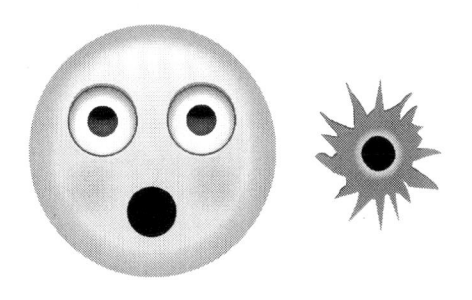

Gun Safety

Unfortunately, this has been a hot topic on the news and in social media lately. It seems like too many people just don't know what to do around a gun. For the purposes of this book, it shouldn't matter whether you are pro- or anti-Second Amendment or the right to conceal carry. This chapter is about gun safety and how to behave around them.

I would not consider myself a gun expert by any stretch of the imagination. However, I have been around guns most of my life. I shot them while in Boy Scouts and have owned them ever since.

Anyone looking to get into shooting for any reason would be well advised to register for at least one, if not more, series of lessons from a qualified gun instructor. By going through the class or classes, it will not only boost your confidence as a gun owner but will also increase your skills with one, should you ever need to deploy it.

If you chose to carry a weapon for protection – and that is your right in most states – you should get training in this arena, as well. It is my opinion, and seemingly that of most people who carry for protection, that the last thing they ever want to do is actually have to use it to protect themselves or loved ones around them. But they get training and practice regularly so that if such a need ever does arise, they will be able to use their gun accurately and confidently without having to worry about doing something wrong and suffering the consequences.

Jeff Cooper is a very well-known authority in all manner of gun safety and overall weapons knowledge. I have listed below for his four most important rules of gun safety:

1. Treat every gun as if it were loaded.
2. Never let the muzzle cover anything you are not willing to destroy.
3. Keep your finger off the trigger until your sights are on your target.
4. Be sure of your target and what's behind it.

I hate to hear on the news about a gun accident that occurred because "it went off while I was cleaning it." That is the biggest bunch of malarkey. It went off because the gun handler was being stupid for some reason. And if it made the news, he or she has probably just cost themselves or someone else their life or serious injury.

Never let that person be you!

Common Sense About Your Car

Getting Pulled Over by the Police

If you find yourself being pulled over by the police for any reason, do whatever you can to make the whole affair go as smoothly as possible. Keep in mind that the police officer doesn't want to pull you over any more than you want to be pulled over. They don't know anything about you and are probably just as nervous about it as you may be.

So, here is how you should handle this situation:

- Pull over, off the road, to a place that is safe for both you and the officer. If it's on a highway, pull as far off the shoulder as safely possible.
- Turn off your engine and roll down the windows. If it's nighttime, turn on your dome light so the officer can see inside your car.
- Take off your sunglasses.
- Turn off the radio.
- Keep your hands on the steering wheel where the officer can see them.
- Do not fidget in the car or look for your documents at this time. You should already know where they are. Fidgeting at this time makes it look like you are stashing something. Your behavior may be innocent, but the officer doesn't know anything about you at this point.

If you are legally carrying a firearm in your car, the time to tell him is immediately after the officer introduces themselves. It will probably sound something like this: "Hello, I am Officer Smith of the Highway Department. Do you know why I pulled you over this afternoon?"

Your response should be something like this, "Thank you, Officer Smith. I need to let you know that I have a weapon in my car. How do you want to proceed?"

Most likely he will thank you for letting him know and will give you very direct instructions about how to deal with the weapon, as well as dealing with the reason he pulled you over in the first place.

It may be just a speeding ticket, but it could be something else. You can make the stop go more smoothly by having your documents together, treating him with respect, and not acting like a rude idiot. Chances are good that you might get off with a warning or a greatly reduced ticket simply for being polite and upfront with him.

As the driver of the car, it is your responsibility to keep your documents, such as the registration and insurance card, up to date and in an easily accessible place. Doing so demonstrates to the officer that you are responsible and squared away in this regard. It will also ease your stress to know exactly where they are, instead of frantically searching your car without having a clue. That behavior won't make you look responsible and or squared away in the least.

The most important thing in ensuring that a traffic stop goes smoothly is checking whatever attitude you may have about the police. Flaunting that chip on your shoulder most likely will not serve you well in this situation.

Changing a Tire

There is nothing more upsetting than being excited to set out on a road trip or running late for an important job interview and getting a flat tire. Even with the best laid plans and preparation, shit happens and knowing how to deal with it is half the battle.

It is quite likely that your auto insurance carrier offers a flat repair service and can be dispatched right from your cell phone, without you even having to know what a lug wrench might be.

However, changing a tire is a skill every driver should have because your cell phone won't always be in a coverage zone or your battery could be on 3 percent.

Believe it or not, many modern cars don't even come with a spare anymore – perhaps just a can of Fix-a-Flat®. Don't rely on that to get you out of a tight spot. Fix-a-Flat® can only do so much if your tire has been completely destroyed in a blowout.

If possible and your trunk is large enough, look into getting a full-size spare. Someday, you may be glad you did. Remember to check it regularly, such as when you have your tires rotated as part of your regular car maintenance. The service guy or gal will be happy to do that for you.

Should you find yourself with a flat tire, here is what to do:

- Do not panic, hit the brakes, or swerve your car to get off the road. This is the worst thing you could do and might very well lead to an accident.
- Keep control of your vehicle by easing off the gas and slowly applying the brakes to get your car off the road. The ride won't be smooth and will feel a little funny, but the other three tires will continue to support the car.

- If you need to drive a bit farther to pull off safely, do that; the tire is already dead and you can't save it. As long as you go slowly, you won't damage the rim.

Make sure you pull your car to the safest and flattest location available. If you're on a highway shoulder, use immense caution before getting out to check the car to see what the damage might be. Check your surroundings for your safety, as well. If you have road service like AAA then by all means reach out and make contact with them. Take note of your location and any other identifying factors that will assist the service provider in finding you.

Should fate decide that you will have to change this tire on your own today, these are the steps you'll need to follow:

1. Locate the jack and the tools that go with it.
2. Verify that your spare is in good enough working order to put on the car. If it's not in viable shape, you will have to walk to a place where you can make a phone call.
3. Using the tire iron, loosen but don't remove the lug nuts on the wheel. This is easier while the car is flat on the ground.
4. Most vehicles have a designated jacking location marked underneath the car next to each of the wheels. Take note of these and place the jack in one of those places, according to the manufacturer's instructions.
5. Jack up the car just high enough for the wheel to clear any fenders and come off the road.
6. Now you can remove the previously loosened lug nuts. Keep these in a safe place, as you will need to use them again. You don't want to have to search for them when you're ready to put the spare tire on.
7. Put the spare tire on the rim and replace the lug nuts.
8. Add the lug nuts in a cross pattern, not in a circular pattern. Put the first one on loosely – and then the one across from it. Follow this pattern with the remaining lug nuts. Snug them up but do not tighten them just yet.
9. Lower the car to the ground.
10. Once the car is back on the ground, tighten each nut with the lug wrench, again using the cross pattern instead of a circular pattern.

Now that you are done, take a look around. Attempt to wiggle the wheel to verify that it feels secure. Clean up your mess and ease back on to the road; then find the nearest repair facility. If you have to go farther than a few miles, it is a good idea to pull over again and re-check the lug nuts just to make sure they are secure.

Chances are high that your girlfriend, boyfriend, or friends in general will be impressed by your skills and will ask you to join them on their next road trip. Accomplishing this also deserves pizza and a cold beer –and will make a great adventure story for years to come.

BTW: I would recommend first trying this whole process in your driveway where it's a safe place to learn.

Car Emergency Kit

Every car you own should contain an emergency kit. If planned right, they don't take up much space in the trunk. And, if something happens to you or your car, it could mean saving your life, surviving the event, and/or being discovered more quickly in a remote area.

The container you use to store this in will be up to you. It could be a dedicated backpack, an old ammo container, plastic storage box, etc. The size and form of the container will depend on how complex your kit gets.

Ideally, your kit should contain items to get you through whatever weather you might encounter on a road trip or in your area of the country.

Here are some things your kit should contain:

- Blankets
- Road side flares
- First aid kit (Be sure to keep this up to date, as some items expire.)
- Water, at least one gallon per person
- Energy bars of some sort. (Most have long expiration dates.)
- Waterproof matches and other fire-starting materials
- Sharp knife
- Whistle
- Duct tape
- Good length of string or light rope

Add any other things to the kit you think you might need to get yourself through an emergency.

Driving and Technology

Technology in cars has come a long way from 8-track tapes and manually rolling down the windows in the cars your parents or grandparents drove. Twenty years ago, self-driving cars were a thing of the future – nothing more than the dream or starry-eyed vision of inventor-type folks.

Today, a button or automated computer device has taken the place of many of the things we used to do manually. The cockpits of modern cars now look more like a fighter jet than the old family sedan. Dashboards contain things like head-up displays, blind spot signals, collision alarms, and automatic brakes just in case you are not already paying attention to what you are doing as a responsible driver.

The big challenge is whether or not you can do all of the things your car is now doing for you if those systems somehow fail. Regardless of your backup screen, you still need to know how to turn your head to check behind you – as well as developing all the other skills you should have if you are to be an excellent driver, and just in case those fancy systems were to fail on you in traffic.

No matter how well-equipped your car's technology, it is still your responsibility to drive safely. Faulty equipment or technical failure is no excuse for getting in an accident that could take a life – including your own.

Now that the dad talk is over, let's get down to business!!

Changing Lanes

Try your best to know which lanes you'll need to be in for any upcoming turns as far ahead as reasonably possible. Perhaps this is just a couple of blocks for city driving, yet up to a mile or so in advance for highway and freeway driving.

Check your mirrors and not just the electronic devices that may or may not tell you something is in your blind spot. Use your turn signal to indicate your plan to shift lanes, and make a final check by actually turning your head to visually verify that you are in the clear.

This final head check has saved me from a number of near misses, especially with motorcycles which can be nearly impossible to spot in your mirrors.

Texting and Driving.

We've all seen the commercials about dead kids, the billboards and PSAs, and yet we just can't seem to resist the urge to respond when that phone beeps. Especially if it has to do with tonight's hot date or the latest bit of juicy gossip from the girls. Call it human nature, perhaps. You know how dangerous it is, but you do it anyway.

Your job as a driver is to arrive at your destination as quickly and safely as possible, and also to look out for the safety of those around you. Nothing good comes from an accident, unless you're a lawyer or own a body shop.

Here's something to ponder: Would you be embarrassed by the last text on your phone if it caused you to run into someone?

What would your mom say if she knew?

Is it really urgent enough to risk people's lives – including your own?

Need we say more on this subject?

GPS and Navigation Systems

Automobile navigation has changed quite a bit from the days of a good roadmap or printed TripTiks from AAA. Yet plenty of stories are floating around the internet about how someone blindly followed their GPS and ended up a long way from their intended destination.

If you are traveling to a place you have never been before, it is wise to confirm the route by a map first. Google Maps is a good place to start – but you might want to do this on a screen larger than your phone so you can see the details. Take a good look at the route, identify the surrounding topography, and take note of waypoints along the route. Consider printing the map, or written directions, and taking it with you. Your GPS app or device could go out on you, mid-trip, and you would be stuck if you were solely depending on it to get you to Grandma's house through the forest.

Today's GPS systems are really good at guiding you to your destination by telling you which exits to look for and precisely how far away they are. They often indicate which lane you should be in, sometimes repeating this information more than once. Paying attention and perhaps having a copilot can make the journey that much more fun.

When You're Paying Someone Else to Drive

Uber, Lyft, and other transportation apps and services have forever changed the way some of us get from one place to the next. It seems like a no-brainer to call a driver instead of getting behind the wheel drunk, and studies have shown that drunk driving has decreased in many cities where such ride sharing services are available.

That doesn't mean you still don't need to use some common sense when using one of these services. Here are a few things you can do to stay safe when using an app like Uber or Lyft:

1. Tell someone when you're calling a driver, especially when traveling alone at night. Do this by pressing the "Share My ETA" option on the Uber app and the "Send ETA" option on Lyft.

2. Whenever possible, avoid making yourself a target by remaining indoors to call and wait for your car.

3. Keep your personal details to yourself. If you're an open person, there's no harm in having a friendly conversation with your driver but avoid offering up any personal information like how long you will be traveling, where you live, your phone number, or other contact info.

4. Be sure to rate your driver once you arrive at your destination. This helps the companies keep good drivers behind the wheel and bad ones off the road.

5. Make sure you look for the sticker and confirm your driver's name, license plate number, and the make and model of their car before jumping in. Cases of scammers posing as rideshare drivers have been reported, so confirm the name of the passenger they're picking up before you get inside the car.

6. It's easy to forget or blow off putting on your seatbelt, but you're in a car with a human driver. Don't assume "it'll never happen" to you. Snap that belt as soon as you close the door. Remember that the drivers rate you, too – wearing your seatbelt will help with your rating as an Uber passenger.
7. If you're using a rideshare service in an unfamiliar area, be sure to track your route before you call so that you know the driver is taking you in the right direction. If you're using a rideshare service to pick you up from the airport, always follow the instructions, as prompted, when you open the rideshare app.

Apply the same rules in your own neighborhood if you're calling for a ride when you're alone late at night. When you're calling from a bar, be especially aware and alert as possible.

Common Sense Around the House

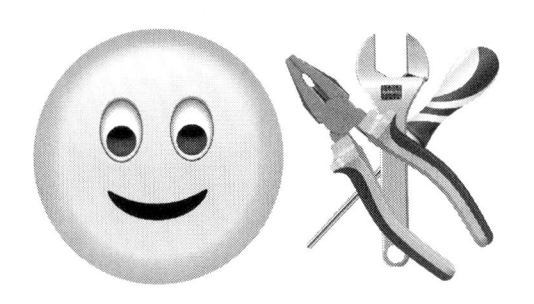

Home Preparedness

If you're just getting out on your own, you are most likely running into these things really quickly or have already had to figure them out the hard way.

Whether it's an apartment you're renting on your own or a house you are sharing with some friends, you will need some basic tools to help you fix, repair, or maintain things.

The local hardware store can be your best friend, so you should get to know it pretty well. The employees there love to help! They've probably been in your situation at least once or twice already, so they know what you are going through.

Everyone – both guys and gals – should have a good tool box at home that contains these basic tools, if not additional ones. This is also an area where you do not want to skimp on quality. Spend the money on quality, reliable products now, and they will last for a very long time.

Your tool box should include:

- Basic hammer
- Set of screwdrivers, both Phillips head (star shape) and standard head (flat) in sizes #1 and #2
- 6-inch adjustable wrench
- 6- or 8-inch channel lock pliers
- Pair of regular pliers
- 25-ft. tape measure
- Set of drill bits
- Couple of rolls of duct tape – which can solve all sorts of problems around the house

- Set of hex wrenches both in metric and standard sizes
- Corded or cordless drill
- Utility knife. Mine is bright green so I can find it easily.
- Assortment of zip ties – which come in handy for all sorts of temporary fixes

Where you take it from there will depend on how handy you are and what tools you might have acquired either by necessity or because you received them as gifts. If money is an issue, estate sales and thrift stores can be great places to purchase used hand tools – but be sure to spend the money for new electric tools like a drill.

A very good habit to get into is creating a space to store your tools and always putting your tools back once you're done using them. This way, you'll be able to find them quickly the next time, when you need them most.

Most weekends, you can find DIY classes at your local hardware or home improvement stores. YouTube is also great for learning how to fix things. It has helped me figure out how to make a number of household repairs over the years.

Your Medicine Cabinet

You may never have had to stock one of these before, since the house where you grew up probably already had one in place. Like it not, however, at some time you will get sick while you're on your own.

No one will be around to take care of you, so you will have to take care of yourself. It's something every adult needs to learn to manage, and as long as you have some good instincts, you should be all right.

You'll need some things in your medicine cabinet besides your chosen cleaning and grooming supplies: items that will help when you get a cut, burn, bug bite, or experience some other household emergency. Having these supplies immediately available in a single place will reduce your panic and make the whole experience less traumatic.

Here are some basic things you'll need, although your personal list might vary based on any health issues that you may be facing.

- Band-Aids of various sizes
- Oral thermometer, either old school or electronic
- Tweezers
- Antiseptic gel or ointment, such as Neosporin
- Anti-itch cream, gel, or spray, such as Benadryl
- Ibuprofen or acetaminophen for headaches and other body aches
- Gauze pads for larger cuts
- Bandage tape for securing those gauze pads in place

You can certainly find a more complete list online or get one from your doctor's office. Remember to update these items periodically, either as you use them or they expire.

It's a good idea to have an emergency stash somewhere of any drugs you may take on a regular basis. This might include a travel kit you stock and store exclusively with your travel gear.

With the rising costs and uncertainty of health care plans these days, you are fully responsible for your health and wellness. If you can take care of a small issue before it becomes a big issue, you will be ahead of the game.

If something does go wrong and you think you need to go to the emergency room, consider urgent care first. They can handle many health issues, and it won't cost as much as a trip to the ER. If your health challenge is truly an emergency, they'll let you know.

That said, in any life-threatening situation, head straight for the ER without hesitating!

Grocery Shopping

When I was about 10, I started going to the store for my mom because, oddly enough, she never learned to drive. So I would ride my bike up to the store with the short list of whatever I could carry on my handlebars. Needless to say, I am pretty good at shopping now and can get through a store pretty quickly and efficiently.

Grocery shopping can a daunting task if you have never really shopped for yourself before. There are all sorts of goodies out there, and you can rack up a hefty bill rather quickly without getting all the things you really need.

Here are some tips to consider:

- Don't go to the store hungry if you can help it. When you shop while your stomach is growling, things seem to jump into your cart that were not on your list.
- Speaking of lists, make one! This is a great way to stay on track – and hopefully within your budget. When making your list, go through the kitchen and the rest of the house to see what is needed for the great meal you are preparing or the items that are running low, like toilet paper, etc. This will prevent you from getting home to find you have forgotten something crucial – it sucks to realize when you're unpacking the groceries that you have to drive back to the store.
- I have never been much of a coupon person, but they can be helpful if you use them wisely. Coupons are designed to entice you to buy things you may not typically use. Make sure you only keep the ones for items you would already want or need. This is where meal planning can coincide with your shopping list. Many stores have apps you can use for additional savings.

- A membership to a bulk discount store *might* be for you. If you have the ability to shop in bulk and properly store these items, you could be well ahead on your overall food budget. A small chest or deep freezer can be your best friend for good buys on meat, chicken, bread, etc. A word of caution, though: these stores are not called $100-dollar stores for no reason. Most people can't get out of them for less than a C-note. This is where your list and a full tummy will really come in handy.
- Most regular grocery stores have fairly competitive pricing, so it normally doesn't make sense to drive to several stores just to save a dollar on a gallon of milk. You will waste more time and gas going here and there than you will save on groceries. The best practice is to choose a store you like and sign up for its rewards program. This will be much easier on your time and hard-earned money. Savings programs at certain grocery stores also accrues savings on gasoline.

Setting Up Your Kitchen

This is another area where having the right tools will make the experience so much nicer.

Here are some tools and implements you will need in your kitchen:

- an 8- or 10-inch frying pan or two (because sometimes you'll need to cook more than one thing at a time)
- a few pots that hold at least 4 or 6 quarts
- a 12-quart stock pot
- a strainer
- a variety of serving utensils (these can often be purchased as a kit during the holidays or online)
- a basic set of silverware
- a can opener (manual or electric)
- a blender (especially useful for smoothies or making your own frappes at home and saving a boatload of money)
- a good set of knives

   A good quality knife will not only stay sharper longer but will be safer to use. Do not skimp here, or your thumb could pay the price later.

- a cooking thermometer (not to be confused with the one in your medicine cabinet)
- a slow cooker (also commonly known as a crock pot)

   This can be your best friend and a great way to make delicious, healthy food while you are away at work. There's nothing like coming home to a house that smells like your mom's favorite stew. Slow cookers are relatively inexpensive and worth exploring. A variety of recipes for everything from chicken to stew to pot roast can be found in a booklet that comes with your new crock pot, in your favorite bookstore, or online.

You will also want a way to store food and pack lunches. These items will help:

- rolls of aluminum foil and plastic wrap
- a variety of zipper storage bags
- a good assortment of plastic food storage containers

    You can save money and help the environment by reusing the containers for things like sour cream and yogurt.

Next, you'll want to stock your pantry. Get what works for you, but some basics include:

- rice
- dried pasta and noodles
- beans (dried or canned)
- canned tomatoes
- canned tuna
- canned coconut milk
- canned soup
- chicken broth
- bread
- peanut butter
- cereal
- snacks (nuts, dried fruit, crackers, pretzels)
- cooking oil
- vinegar (white, balsamic, apple cider, white wine)
- soy sauce or tamari
- honey
- syrup
- all-purpose flour
- sugar
- coffee and tea

You'll probably want to season your food. Consider including these spices on your shopping list:

- pepper
- salt
- garlic
- rosemary
- thyme
- cumin
- cinnamon

Pick up any other items you might like along the way.

You may find that you receive or inherit many of the kitchen tools and gadgets as you move out, or you can purchase them as you need them for various recipes and dishes you decide to try.

Ready, Set, Cook!

If you didn't learn to cook while at home, now is going to be a good time to figure it out, for a few good reasons.

It's a lot less expensive to fix your meals at home than to eat out every night. Just eating lunch out during your workweek can easily run to $50 per week or $200 a month. Add a fast food dinner every few days and you're in for some big bucks, not to mention that it's one of the quickest ways to pack on the pounds.

As a single person, it can be pretty easy to drop $100 on dinner out with friends or on a date. That same $100 could easily cover a week or two of groceries at home. If you plan well, you don't have to eat ramen noodles every night like you did in college. Steak, chicken, pasta, etc. are all possible if you budget and plan your meals well.

When cooking at home, you can also cook as healthily as you want to because you get to control of what goes into and out of the pan. Your average restaurant meal contains upward of 1,200 calories, about half the recommended caloric intake for adults for the entire day.

Who knows – you might even decide that you like cooking! It's also a great way to destress when you've had a tough day at work and don't feel like going out and being social.

Learning to Cook

You can get started with cooking lessons in a number of ways:

1. If you are a hands-on learner, learning from a friend or family member can be a great way to learn to cook. Talk to them and have them show you a few things.
2. YouTube is a wealth of information for everything from basic recipes

to advanced cooking techniques.

3. If you would rather learn from a chef or someone of the like, classes at your local cooking school or community college might be well worth your time. A class might also be a great way to meet people or something fun to do on a date.

The most important thing to remember is that you will not be a chef right out of the gate. Even the best chefs in the world have burned a few dinners and called for pizza later. Don't worry about it – and you may have a good story to tell after the fire alarm stops bleating.

Theme Nights

Theme nights with your friends can be a fun way to cook and save money on going out. Taco, spaghetti, or hamburger nights can be fun and easily made into a potluck. Ask everyone to bring something and swap recipes if you like them. Make this time even more special by putting your phones away for a while and enjoying each other's company and food.

Leftovers

Keep in mind that most recipes are designed for four or more servings. You will more than likely be cooking for yourself, maybe two people. Depending on what you make, using a recipe could work out for leftovers or multiple meals out of the same pot. Spaghetti and other Italian dishes make for good leftovers and are sometimes even better the second day. Stews, casseroles, and chili also tend to fall into this category. Fried foods generally don't do well the second day.

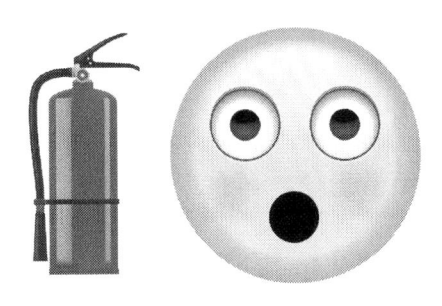

Fire Extinguishers and Smoke Alarms

A chapter on home preparedness would be incomplete without a discussion of fire extinguishers and smoke alarms.

These are some of the most basic and effective safety tools in any home or apartment.

The ideal placement for smoke alarms is outside sleeping rooms, in the living room, and in the kitchen. In the kitchen, be sure place it no less than 10 feet from the cooking area to prevent false alarms. In the other rooms, it should not be directly in front of the HVAC vents, as your AC or heating unit could cause accidentally trigger the alarm at the wrong time.

Many higher quality alarms will have dual sensors and a sealed battery. This means it will be more responsive and usually good for about 10 years. It makes sense to buy the best you can afford, as you and your family's life may depend on it someday.

You should regularly test your smoke alarms to make sure they are working properly. Once a month is ideal. This is also a good time to give them a quick dusting with a damp microfiber towel and also do a quick blowout of the vents.

For your fire extinguishers, it is certainly ideal to have one in the kitchen that is rated for all types of fires, including grease and oil fires. You should also have one in the garage near a common entry/exit and also rated for all types of fires.

Your fire extinguisher should be mounted on the wall using the brackets provided. Make sure you have easy access to it but avoid putting it in a place where it could be knocked around during regular household traffic.

Good quality fire extinguishers usually have gauges on them, so you can tell if they are still serviceable and in good working order. It makes sense to check these on the same schedule as your monthly smoke alarm testing. This is not an area where you want to skimp on your safety.

If you have never used a fire extinguisher, your local fire department will be happy to give you a demonstration and help you learn the basics. Call ahead to schedule an appointment with them. If you have some friends who would also like to learn this, get them all together and go in a group.

This would also be a good activity for a club, fraternal group, team building activity, etc.

Should you find yourself ever needing to use your fire extinguisher, the first thing is not to panic. Take the extinguisher off the rack, pull the safety pin, and aim the stream at the base of the fire. Then sweep across to cover the burning area. If this is not enough to douse the fire, back away and call 911 as quickly as possible. If you have the ability to close the doors to this room, do so. This may help keep it from spreading any faster than it needs to.

Pest Control and Creepy Crawlies

Basic pest control in your home or apartment begins with making sure that it is neat and clean, with no food lying about. Ants, roaches, and crickets are no fun to worry about and tend to keep friends and guests from visiting you.

Make sure your doors and window seals are in good condition and working properly. If you are in an apartment, an easy call to the manager should be all it takes to arrange the service request. If you're not renting, it's an easy trip to the local hardware store and a couple of hours of your time. Proper window and door seals will also help keep your home weather tight. Who wants to air condition the outdoors?

A number of pest control products are available on the grocery store or hardware store shelves today. The type you need depends on the kinds of creepy crawlies you have in your house.

<u>Ants</u>

Ants usually have discovered some sort of food source and come in from the outside. Just follow the path back to the source. Clean it up and hit them with some good ant spray. Then seal the hole where they came in, and you should be good to go.

<u>Roaches</u>

When I die and get to heaven, the first question I ask God will be, "What the hell is with the roaches, Man?" These bugs are also attracted to food and can certainly be scary looking. It is common for them to come up through drains and other water sources. Keep your drains clean and clear. Also make sure you have traps and strainers in place to keep the roaches where they belong and out of your house.

If you do find you have an infestation of any kind, it's a good idea to call a reputable pest control company.

Bees

Bees generally won't cause too much of a problem. The only time you should be concerned is when you see or hear a bunch of them. They are most active when the weather warms up in spring and summer. Swarms and hives can appear just about anywhere and should only be handled by bee professionals.

Should you encounter a swarm of bees, run as quickly as possible in a straight line to an indoor shelter, such as a house or a car. Close the doors and windows to keep them out.

Contrary to popular belief, jumping in a pool will not keep bees away. They will just hover around until you come up for air. It's quite possible that they will hover longer than you can hold your breath.

One or two bee stings should not harm most healthy people. If you are allergic or get stung multiple times, it is wise to seek professional medical attention. The local fire department usually will respond very quickly to bee calls.

Common Sense About Your Money

The Importance of Credit

Now that you are out on your own – or nearly there – one of the most important things you can do is start to build your credit history. Although this may not sound as exciting as some of the other topics, it will be one of the most crucial to master over your lifetime.

Credit is an important tool and can be quite helpful, as long as you use it properly. A credit card will allow you to rent cars, reserve hotel rooms, and purchase plane tickets to far-away places. It can also be useful for business and emergencies.

However, if you use it irresponsibly, your credit can go bad quicker than a puppy video gone viral. Credit card debt has been a major contributor to Americans' filing for bankruptcy for many years.

How Credit Works

- Your bank issues you a credit card for, let's say, a $1,000 limit.
- You can spend up to that limit.
- Once you've spent it, though, you have to pay it back – with interest. As of this writing, the average credit card interest rate is 16.8%. That means for every $100 of credit you borrow, you have to pay an extra $16.80 before that debt is considered paid off. This is how banks and credit card companies make their money – the money you spend on credit is really a loan, and those loans all come with interest.
- Your monthly statement will show the minimum amount you must pay. Most of that payment will be interest, not principal.
- This cycle repeats every 30 days, whether you pay the minimum or more.

Building Your Credit History

It takes four things to properly build a healthy credit history:

1. Make your payments on time consistently.
2. Pay more than the minimum payment.
3. Keep your balance to 50% of the maximum limit.
4. Use it, pay it off, use it, pay it off, etc.

How will your credit history affect your life? Many companies will use it to qualify you for to purchase a new car or a new house, rent an apartment, or qualify for employment. Yes – many employers do credit checks before they hire their staff. I cannot stress enough how important it is to pay attention to this part of your life, starting NOW!

Car Payments versus Housing Payments

As a loan officer for 10 years, I have seen my share of home loans get denied because the borrower's car loan was more than the proposed house payment, making their debt-to-income ratio higher than the maximum limit allowed. Having this discussion with a prospective borrower is never fun.

Imagine a young person just out of college working at his or her first professional job. They're feeling great to be earning real money, and the dealership salesperson talks them into a sports car because they "deserve it" for making it through college and landing this great job.

They also need to find a place to live that doesn't remind them of their dorm room.

Currently, rent for the average 2-bedroom apartment in the U.S. runs nearly $1,200 per month. Add in the $700/month payment for that Mustang, now we're looking at an annual expense of more than $ 20,000, just for home and transportation. Not to mention all the other things that are about to start coming due: lights, water, gas, food, phone, internet, insurance –oh yes, and those college loans.

One course not required as part of any college or university curriculum is personal finance. This is a damn shame. All the calculus and trigonometry you may have studied will not balance your checkbook for you. Truthfully, how often have you used your calculus knowledge since you passed that class, anyway?

If you have not left university yet, please do yourself a huge favor and enroll in a consumer math class. In it, you will learn all about personal finance, from how to manage your checking account to how credit works to how to understand loans and interest rates. Most importantly, you will learn how to create a budget based on your income and how to live within it.

I grew up in a world where the most important thing was being reliable and being able to report to work on time. Doing this means have a reliable car, not necessarily the fanciest ride on the block. Not to mention that fancy rides break down, too – and they cost a pretty penny to repair.

College may be over, so yes, you should be able to live a little higher on the hog if possible. But unless your car is making you money, it's a depreciating asset, meaning that the minute you drive it off the lot, you will sell it for a lot less than you paid for it.

Only you can determine your living standards. Whatever you do, make every effort to manage your money and lifestyle wisely. Your parents love you, but they probably aren't so eager for you to move back home now that they've turned your room into a personal gym, craft room, or office.

If you have already graduated from college, all the more reason for you to master financial literacy. Plenty of tools are available to help you create a budget and learn about personal finance. Find a resource to help you, be it online, through your local credit union, or a personal finance coach.

Budgets and Spending

One of the most important thing to get a handle on quickly is the management of your money, both incoming (earning) and outgoing (spending).

An easy way to keep things in check is to make sure you pay your bills first, then save even a little play money, while important, comes last. Your bills most likely will include:

- Rent
- Renter's insurance
- Utilities
- Phone/internet
- Car payment
- Car insurance
- Gas and auto maintenance
- Student loan
- Food

You can handle some of these things electronically or on your phone. However, keeping track of the big picture sometimes works better when you lay it all out in front of you on paper – or even an Excel spreadsheet.

Building a good financial foundation starts with creating the habit of paying your bills on time. Starting off on the right foot now will help you build a solid credit profile. On-time bill paying makes up a very large portion of your overall credit profile, because it indicates the likelihood you will reliably pay off loans for cars, homes, etc. Creating a strong credit profile now will increase your chances of receiving more favorable terms when you apply for credit in the future.

As a loan officer, I have seen many a young person with a car payment that's higher than their rent payment. This is backwards from what it should be. According to Maslow's Hierarchy of Needs, food, water, and air are a person's first-level needs (physiological), followed by shelter (safety). The fancy car comes later on.

This is not to say that you don't deserve – or can't have – a fancy ride; however, it is more important that your first car out of the gate be safe, reliable, and won't cost you a fortune to keep up.

At this early point in your career, it might be a good idea to speak with a Certified Financial Planner (CFP) in person, to get have them help you craft a plan for the next 5 to 10 years.

While we are on the subject of money, let's chat about saving, for a moment. Learning how to save money is an important skill – one at which most Americans have a nearly 0.0 batting average. If your parents didn't instill this habit in you as a child, it's no wonder we often have a difficult time establishing this life-changing behavior.

Savings will come in handy for emergencies, planned trips, large purchases and, of course, retirement. You probably can't even imagine that far into the future but believe me when I tell you it will be here before you know it, and you most definitely don't want to find yourself wishing you'd started earlier when you've only got a couple thousand dollars in the bank as you're about to turn 65 (or whatever the retirement age may be when you get there).

One of the easiest ways to begin saving is by electing to have a certain amount of money deducted from your paycheck every pay period, and have those funds go directly into a separate savings account. This is known as a payroll deduction. If you set it up from the beginning, you won't even miss this small amount from your regular paycheck, and it will be there in the background for when the need arises.

If your employer matches your 401(k) contributions, you should put as much into that account as you can afford. Then don't look at it more than maybe once a year. The funds in this account will most likely build faster than you realize. I am not a stock broker or any sort of financial advisor, but any good financial planner will tell you: "Your goal is time in the market, not timing the market." That means save consistently now, rather than trying to bet on the next hot stock tip.

Tipping

Many articles have been written on the art and practice of tipping in restaurants and other service-related fields. While it is not a common practice in many other countries, tipping is the norm here in America. Perhaps you've even worked a job where most of your income came from tips.

There are many situations where tipping for good quality service is expected or highly recommended, whether it be in a restaurant or to a driver, a bellman, the housekeeper in your hotel, or the person who cuts and styles your hair. Fifteen percent is generally accepted as the bare minimum, while 20 percent or more is the standard for good service. You can find plenty of apps for smartphones to help you determine the amount of the tip, based on the total cost of the product or service.

Many people who work at jobs that earn tips make the majority of their income from their tips – for some of them, tips make up as much as 70 percent of their income. Sure, it might be their chosen profession, but it could also be a position they just happen to find themselves in right now. Any way you look at it, this job – and their tips – is how they're putting food on the table for themselves and their family. They most likely are working hard to make sure you have a good experience with your family and friends, so remember to take care of them, in return.

If the food is bad, don't blame the server or stiff them on their tip; they didn't prepare your meal, they just served it to you. You'd want to speak with the manager about the food quality. It also doesn't help to be rude when you're trying to settle a matter of poor service – in any situation, not just at a restaurant. Things happen (cooks get sick, orders don't come in on time, life) and sometimes service providers miss the mark. Your being rude or nasty isn't going to make things any better. As a matter of fact, if you are polite while drawing attention to the problem (also known as making a complaint), the manager will be much more likely to comp your meal or offer you a free dessert.

Tipping the Bellman

Back in the day when I worked as a bellman, the norm was to tip a dollar or two per bag. Today the rate is between $1 and $5 per bag, depending on the place and caliber of hotel. The size of the tip might depend on how far we had to schlep the bag, any help or suggestions we might provide along the way about things to do in the hotel or city during the guest's visit, etc. All of this played a part in the amount of the tip.

My goal was always to get at least $5 per guest I helped. If I had 20 check-ins that night, I wanted to take home a minimum of $100 in cash that per night. Not a bad night. Some nights, I earned more than $200 – even better! I went home tired but got to eat a little better.

Tipping Your Hairdresser

Whether your hair guy or gal owns the salon or just rents a booth there, they are still providing a personal service to you, and they deserve a tip for that. Your standard should be 20 percent of the bill. If a different person shampoos your hair, they generally receive about $5.

Tipping the Hotel Housekeeper

Staying at a hotel is fun and you don't have to clean up after yourself. However, someone does – and if you wouldn't want to clean up after yourself, imagine how the cleaning staff feels, especially if you leave your room a hurricane-wrought disaster. Housekeeping may not be their dream job, but it's what they're doing at the moment to make a living, and you can help make their job just a bit easier.

A hotel room is not your home, and it's impolite to toss your stuff – including dirty underwear – around for them to pick up. If you choose to have daily service during your stay, it is customary to leave a few bucks for the housekeeping staff every day. If you like, you can cancel the daily service and just have them come when you check out. Depending on the length of your stay, your tip at checkout should be at least $5. An envelope is often left in the room just for this purpose.

Tipping the Valet

Driving up to a restaurant or hotel and simply dropping off your car without having to park it is a luxury. The valet has to get into your car, no matter how tidy or untidy you keep it, figure out how to operate it without changing your mirror, seat, or steering wheel settings, and park it for you somewhere. Sometimes they do this during the freezing cold or blazing heat. And they generally hustle to make sure you don't wait any longer than is necessary.

You should tip the valet at least $2 when you drop your car off and $5 when you pick it up.

Tipping the Delivery Driver

These are hardworking folks, just like you. They drive around at odd hours of the night just to bring pizza, Chinese, or whatever you might order from Grubhub, to your front door. – so you don't have to cook or drive. When it comes to tipping the delivery guy or gal, I generally base it on 20 percent of the bill, or a minimum of at least $5.

Tipping for your Uber, Lyft, or Taxi Driver

It is customary to offer a tip of some amount to anyone who provides this service to you. Short rides might only warrant $1 to $2 per person. Drivers for longer or more complex trips might deserve closer to 20 percent of the total fare. These guys work hard for their money, so be nice to them.

Remember that the tipping is built into the app for Uber and Lyft – there's no need ever to tip those drivers in cash. On the other hand, I know people who've had their credit card numbers stolen when they paid taxi drivers by card – so you might want to pay and tip traditional cab drivers in cash.

It all comes down to this: service industry folks work hard to make sure you have a good time – and you should take care of them for this. If you have never spent any time working in service industry, try it, even if briefly. You might just learn a lot about how to work with people, how to hustle, and about common courtesy.

It's a thrill to know that your service for someone totally made their night – or experience.

Hiring Contractors, Mechanics, and Other Service Providers

You quite often see stories on the news about a person who was scammed out of some serious money by a con artist or fake provider. The question that never seems to come up is: "Did you check them out before hiring them?"

So how do you protect yourself in these situations? Simple: perform your due diligence – that is, research the prospective service provider before paying them a penny. Check them out with friends and family, check out their websites, and read their Yelp reviews. Also check with the Better Business Bureau, the local attorney general, and the licensing board they should be affiliated with. Yes, this can be a bit time consuming. But you work hard for your money – so do you really have the time lose it or get tangled up in a scam? I didn't think so.

First, learn about what's involved in the job you are looking to hire out. This way you will know what the prospective provider is talking about and be able to ask solid questions about their process and what you can expect during the experience.

Next, ask them for references and a bid. Smart shoppers get a couple of bids – they don't just hire the first person. If you find yourself uncomfortable with any part of what the prospective provider is telling you, walk away! The lowest bidder isn't necessarily the best provider to hire. You've probably heard that you get what you pay for. That's never truer than in a service business like a mechanic or builder.

Do not pay in cash unless you already know the service provider. This is very important. If they ask for the first half in cash upfront to get started, walk away. Once you pay the provider in cash, they may never come back. And if they rip you off, you will have no way to prove the payment.

Use a credit card (not a debit card) or pay with a check. And pay only a down payment for the full job upfront. Any reputable provider will be happy to provide a complete bill at the end of the job.

It's important that you keep good records, take pictures throughout the process, and perhaps track your communications with the service provider, as you could need this documentation later to support an insurance claim or for a small claims appearance in court.

Finding a good contractor, plumber, electrician, and handyman will come in handy and valuable, should you run into a problem and need someone reliable.

General Life Skills

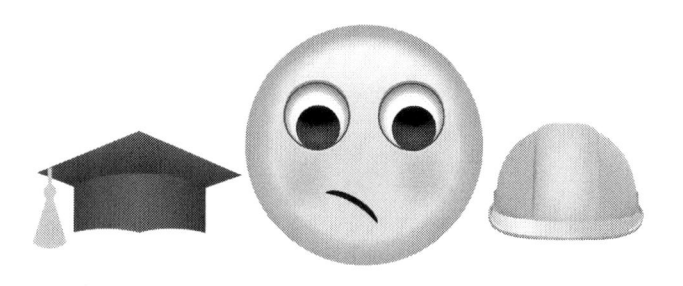

Trade School or University?

For years and years, American parents have dreamed of seeing their kids become doctors, lawyers, and businessmen and women. They've even mortgaged their homes and raided their retirement accounts to make sure those dreams came true.

Years ago, I asked a good friend of mine, "What if your son wanted to become a plumber?" She about fell off her bike, midride. "Absolutely not, not my kid." What a strange reaction. Is there something wrong with being a plumber? Is it not noble, honest work that pays extraordinarily well?

There is nothing more admirable than a hard day's work and well-earned wages. Yet skilled trades are starting to die off because many of those working them are now retiring, and no one is coming up through the ranks to replace them.

Here's something to think about: When all of today's plumbers and builders and electricians are gone, who is going to do those jobs, since your parents thought it was beneath you do plumbing or carpentry or electrical work? And that attitude has been passed down. It's not just parents who didn't want their kids to take blue-collar jobs – young people today won't work in those fields because they perceive it as beneath them. Hundreds of thousands of jobs are going unfilled across the country because no one wants to do "that kind of work."

Who are you going to call at 2 a.m. when water is spouting from your kitchen faucet and you have no clue how to stop it? What's that bill going to look like when you factor in water damage and replacement of flooring, furniture, etc.?

Funny thing is, there's a good chance most of those jobs would pay better than your office job, leave you with less student loan debt, and allow you the ability to have much more fun. Take a look around at your neighbors and see who has the boats and campers in their garages.

Some of these skills are learned in trade schools; the rest comes through on-the-job training. You might work as an apprentice for someone while you learn the ropes and the business. But the ultimate plan would be to work for yourself. It's also quite possible that trade school would cost a whole lot less and be faster than four years at a university.

One other thing to consider is that these jobs and the attendant skills are portable: you can take them with you wherever you go. There is most likely a need for these services in just about any city or town you might want to live in.

Common Courtesy and Manners

Basic Good Manners

I spoke with a young man who works in my office about this book. When I asked him what kinds of behaviors he is seeing or not seeing among his peers, he told me that chivalry, common courtesy, and manners seem to be severely lacking among them.

I was shocked to hear that, seeing that my parents raised us in the Southern tradition of "Yes ma'am, no sir." Good manners are really easy to demonstrate (e.g., saying "please" and "thank you" and looking people in the eye when they speak to you) and make a great statement about yourself when your peers are not behaving this way.

Basic Good Handshake

It is vitally important that you have a good handshake when meeting anyone, guys or gals. There is nothing worse than shaking hands with someone whose handshake is so weak that you think you might be handling a dead, sweaty fish.

Be confident, stick your hand out there, grip firmly, shake once, and release. You don't have to have a grip contest. This is not the place for that kind of behavior. A good handshake does take a little practice, but you will get the hang of it quickly.

The recipient of a fishy handshake may not say anything or give their reaction away on their face, but they will automatically think less of you. Don't blow a good professional relationship or job prospect by handing anyone a sweaty fish.

Basic Polite Behavior

It never hurts you to hold open a door for someone else, whether it be a lady, a mom with her hands full of squirmy kids, an elderly person, or someone with a handicap of some sort. Think about it – you would want someone to do that for your family member if they were in the same predicament, wouldn't you. You will likely be paid back with a smile and a thank you. It may sound old fashioned, but you'll really get people's attention if you stand and/or remove your hat when a woman or older person enters a room.

Basic Polite Conversation

With everybody constantly with their noses in their phones, it seems that many folks today have forgotten how to participate in a real conversation with others. This is a skill that is perishable if not practiced regularly. Take a look around your favorite coffee shop or café. Chances are high that most people are on their phones, not talking with each other, even if they are sitting at a table together. Have you seen parents using their phones as babysitters for their children, instead of engaging them in conversation?

There is something so rewarding about having a face-to-face chat with someone – far more than texting or even talking on the phone. You can see their reactions and responses to the things you are saying. And absolutely nothing can replace the lovely sound of someone laughing at your jokes. This is something emojis just can't duplicate. Yes, we have Facetime and Facebook Live – but video will never capture the true energy and vitality of that other person the way that sitting across from them will.

So, here's a little challenge for you: get together with some friends at a café or someone's house. Then put down your phones and talk with each other. Do a puzzle or play a board game. But turn off the devices, TV included, and get to know each other. Don't just phone it in.

Volunteering

Volunteering can be a great way to spend some of your time helping others. The trick is to find a group or cause you believe in or care about. The most important thing any charitable organization wants is your time – yep, sometimes even more than money. At this writing, it is estimated that the average hour offered by a volunteer saves an organization $24.69 that they'd have to pay someone (including benefits) to do the same work.

Here are some of the things you might gain from giving back to your community:

- You get to help others, which is a great feeling all in itself.
- You can make some quality – and perhaps even lifelong – friends.
- You might learn some valuable job and life skills.
- You can make some valuable business connections. It's not unheard of to find your next job this way.
- You might even have some fun adventures and/or go places you hadn't considered before.

Here are a few suggestions of some (but not nearly all) of the volunteer opportunities available to you:

- American Red Cross
- Big Brothers/Big Sisters
- Local food banks
- Animal rescues and shelters
- Your place of worship
- Hospitals or senior care facilities

If none of these appeals to you, the website VolunteerMatch.org is a great resource for finding the perfect volunteer opportunity. You can use the search fields to indicate your interests, hours of availability, location, and other details to help you find an organization or opportunity that can use your time and talents.

Pet Care

So, you think you'd like a pet. They are fun to have around and make great companions. There is nothing like coming home to see them eagerly waiting for you, tails wagging. If you've had a bad day, they can listen to you rant about things your boss shouldn't hear. The best thing is that they can't repeat any of it. :)

Before you run to the local animal shelter, you must factor your new companion's care and well-being into your expense budget. Here are few additional things you might consider:

If you are renting an apartment or house, will pets be allowed by the landlord? If so, is there a size or weight limit, and possibly specific type of pet permitted?

Next, find a veterinarian you can get to know and with whom you can develop a working relationship. Your best bet will be a vet with a private practice, rather one inside a pet store. You will find this person invaluable when you need good advice and care. A vet you know well will usually take good care of you on your regular visits.

It is also important to buy the best food you can afford for your pet. Do your research, because this matters. You pet will digest higher quality food better, and it will help with controlling their weight and make their poop easier to clean up.

If you get a dog, good training is essential – not only for you, but also for the safety and happiness of the dog. The better trained they are, the more enjoyable they are in social settings and around other people and animals.

Wrapping Up

Woo-hoo!! You are officially an adult now. You have your own car, your own job, and your own place.

Now what??

There will be many things to think about and keep up with. If you made a list, it might look overwhelming at times. However, you can manage all of it with a little planning and organization. Not every monthly task needs to be done in one day. That's just crazy talk there.

You might think about getting a large monthly calendar and sketching out your month, including dates when bills are due, rent, obligations, cleaning, etc.

I am a huge fan of lists and love scratching things off of my daily list when they are done.

Lots of people in your community are just trying to get by, same as you. You might be having a bad day, thus the headphones stuck in your ears while you try to drown out the world by keeping your nose stuck to your phone. That may work for a little while, but not for too long.

Remember that other folks might also be having the worst day ever, and a little human kindness goes a very long way to improving almost anyone's day. Your act of kindness, a smile coupled with a sincere "how ya doing?", holding the door for them, or even allowing them to go ahead of you in the grocery line could make all the difference in their world.

It doesn't cost you a dime to be nice and courteous. And there's a good chance your generous act will come back to you somewhere down the road in a big way, just when you need it most.

Keep these things in mind one day when you have children of your own. If you don't teach the next generation the manners and common courtesies you expect, how will they treat you when you get to be old?

Made in the USA
San Bernardino, CA
08 August 2018